A N A M E R I C A N C I T Y

PITTSBURGH

ALCOA

A N   A M E R I C A N   C I T Y

PITTSBURGH

Photography by Walt Urbina

Text by Sally Webb

Design by Michael Maskarinec

First Published 1990
in Pittsburgh by Urbina Publishing
1113 East Carson St. Pittsburgh, PA 15203

Designed by Michael Maskarinec
Text by Sally Webb

412-242-5070 412-481-9650.

Library of Congress Catalog Card Number (90-71381)
ISBN (0-9627857-0-9) (Paperback pb)
ISBN (0-9627857-1-7) (hc)

Printed in Hong Kong.

Cover separation and composite by Laser Images Inc.

CONTENTS

HILTON
Convention Ctr
Strip District
Liberty Ave
Civic Arena
376
Monroeville

TUNNEL VISION

Pittsburgh makes an impression on first-time visitors that is not easily forgotten .

Enter the city by way of the Fort Pitt Tunnel. Rushing through the glaring white ceramic-tiled walls, the traffic noises bounce about in quadrophonic sound until, quite suddenly, you reach the end and explode into the panoramic vision that is Pittsburgh.

Here, tall shimmering glass and chrome skyscrapers glow in the fading sunset. Here the city reaches upward to claim a magnificence all its own — the pointed towers of the PPG castle, the lofty mast rising from Fifth Avenue Place, the amber glow of lights within the tall USX Tower.

Below, the waters of the Allegheny and Monongahela rivers hug the bank of this downtown urban center, blending together at the Point to form the mighty Ohio. The moving water reflects yellow girded bridges and the graceful lit arcs of the Smithfield Street Bridge.

The Pittsburgh skyline from the Fort Pitt Tunnel.

Fifth Avenue Place at twilight.

St. John the Baptist.

The Towers of PPG Place.

A pleasure craft cuts through the smooth water. It passes a chugging tug, headed upstream, nosing high-floating barges. Around the bend churns an elegant riverboat — a celebration in sight and sound.

And you're only now crossing the bridge, just entering the cosmopolitan scene, barely glimpsing the details of this overpowering vista, still catching your breath.

May we introduce the glittering jewel of a city that can only be called: Pittsburgh.

RECREATION

Year round, Pittsburgh offers play time excitement, and people who know how to have fun.

Picture a hot August afternoon. You're strolling along a boardwalk in a bathing suit and rubber thongs. You pause to watch a beachfront volleyball game. The sand is flying from a point-saving dive for the ball. A warm breeze gently lifts your hair as you sip your frozen cocktail and move on to the pool.

Imagine yourself at a Florida resort? Why, perish the thought, you're practically in your own backyard — Sandcastle, Pittsburgh's wildest and wettest summer playground.

Pittsburgh has long carried a reputation for hard work and drive, but when it comes to free time, the city knows how to play hard too. And when it comes to hot fun in the sun, Sandcastle is one of Pittsburgh's best bets.

Flop into a rubber inner tube for a drift down the Lazy River. The truly adventurous will thrill to the 60-foot high Lightening Express, one of the parks 15 water slides.

Sandcastle, Pittsburgh's waterslide park.

Parade on South Side.

ANDY YOURISH

Thunderbolt rollercoaster at Kennywood Park.

Accordion player performing in ethnic festivities.

More traditional thrill seekers follow the crowd to historic Kennywood Park. Founded in 1907, the amusement park is a fond memory of virtually every Pittsburgher's childhood. With tree-lined walkways, a challenging midway, picnic pavilions, and specialty Kiddieland rides, the park is a favorite family retreat.

But don't let its age deceive you; as the roller coaster capitol of the world, Kennywood's Thunderbolt (named by the *New York Times* as the number one best), Jackrabbit, and Racer, enthuse roller coaster fans from across the country.

Or try a parade. Pittsburgh has a year long schedule to keep you entertained. From the smaller, community-oriented variety to the full-scale productions — like the Celebrate the Season Parade, heralding Santa's arrival into town — all of Pittsburgh loves a parade. Crowds are growing in record numbers each year.

Several parades are ethnic in style. The Columbus Day Parade, held in October, recognizes a strong Italian heritage. And one of the oldest parades in town, the St. Patrick's Day Parade — a tradition that began in Civil War times — brings out the best of the Irish. Downtown's Fifth Avenue is decorated with Kelly green shamrocks, painted along the center line, and local taverns even get into the act, selling green beer on tap for the occasion.

Looking for major league fun? Make a stop in to see the battling Bucs, our own Pittsburgh Pirates, for baseball under the stars. As the seasons change, you can catch the gridiron drama of the National Football League. The Steelers are working to reclaim their glory years, building a new team with high hopes for the future. Hockey, too, has taken the stage in a big way. The Penguins have skated to the forefront of the National Hockey League with the likes of Mario Lemieux, who has all but rewritten the club's record books.

Pittsburgh Pirates at home in Three Rivers Stadium.

Hot air balloon launch over Market Square.

Pittsburgh Steelers.

Local college and universities offer football and basketball challenges: the Pitt Panthers, Duquesne Dukes, and Robert Morris Colonials, to name a few.

Like to get more actively involved in your recreation time? Go for the gold in the Great Race, held each September. As the fifth largest ten-kilometer race in the country, you can join with 12,000 other runners in the race from Squirrel Hill to Point State Park. Only the hardiest runners will want to attempt the Pittsburgh Marathon, but the whole city makes an appearance to cheer on the 5,000 participants in their 26-mile race through the city each May.

And don't forget the rivers. Between boating, water skiing and game fishing, the three rivers and nearby lakes keep weekenders busy. The largest floating event of the year is the four-day Three Rivers Regatta, held in August. Starting off with a parade, the weekend activities include a spectacular hot air balloon launch, Formula One speedboat races, the rubber ducky race, the "Anything That Can Float" competition, and a carnival atmosphere that's sure to coax a smile.

Gateway Clipper Fleet docked at Station Square.

Civic Arena.

Pittsburgh Marathon runners crossing 16th Street Bridge.

North Park Lake.

Lunchtime concert at Mellon Square.

When the rivers start to chill and a frost is in the air, ski buffs needn't travel far from town. Three resorts are within an hour's drive — Seven Springs, Hidden Valley, and the Laurel Mountain Valley. But don't discount local parks, where cross country skiing can be enjoyed.

After the spring thaw, take your chances with heart-stopping whitewater rafting at nearby Ohiopyle State Park. The rushing water moves best at that time of year for a breathtaking ride.

Even duffers can't complain about the area; Pittsburgh has more golf courses per capita of any major city.

As a recreational wonderland through all seasons, Pittsburgh can't be beat. The changes in weather simply mean more varied choices to match everyone's style of fun.

Honus Wagner, Three Rivers Stadium.

Last snow of winter.

Fourth of July fireworks at Point State Park.

ARCHITECTURE

From the old to the new, Pittsburgh landmarks add to the city's beauty.

Pittsburgh's exquisite beauty and charm lie in its complex variation and diversity. Its skyline has never rested for long. Renaissance after renaissance has left its mark on the city's silhouette with more dramatic contrasts and soaring heights.

The most recent flurry of construction gave the city the Art Deco topped CNG Tower and the challenging design of the Liberty Center, whose architect had to contend with a five-view building. One Oxford Center utilizes octagonal geometric patterns, while Fifth Avenue Place creates its impression with cascading emerald glass. And, of course, the mirrored PPG Place, covering five and one-half acres, made a significant contribution to Pittsburgh architecture as well.

Pittsburgh bridges deserve at least as much credit for the celebrated city view. World-class bridge builders have been drawn to Pittsburgh to measure up to the engineering challenge, and have left behind technological wonders. The more than 700 bridges in the city have been designed with every type of arched span, ornamental piers, flowing suspension, trusses and chords.

Gulf Building, Koppers Building, and USX Tower beyond the Sixth Street Bridge.

Downtown beyond the Fort Pitt Bridge.

Fifth Ave. Place.

PPG Place.

Allegheny County Courthouse and Jail.

City County Building.

Not as towering, but just as important to Pittsburgh's image, was the rehabilitation of Heinz Hall, the first step in building downtown's cultural district. It became the new home to the Pittsburgh Symphony Orchestra. Soon to follow was the restoration of the old Stanley Theater, transformed into the Benedum Center for the Performing Arts. The hall retains its 1920s look with the dark wood interior, and a six-ton amber crystal chandelier. The Benedum provides the stage for the Pittsburgh Ballet Theater, as well as the Pittsburgh Opera Company.

The Allegheny County Courthouse and Jail has been claimed as one of the favorite buildings in town. With the look of a Renaissance castle, the large granite blocks contribute further to its aura of strength and power. And as a practical, functioning building, it couldn't have been designed any better.

One of the most extraordinary buildings is the University of Pittsburgh's Cathedral of Learning. The 42-story Gothic skyscraper was completed in 1937 and still towers over Oakland as a symbol of "higher education." The ground floor's Nationality Rooms add even more — each room is designed in the ethnic tradition of the sponsoring country.

Another impressive university building is the 1937 Carnegie Mellon Research Institute, part of Carnegie Mellon University, a classical-revival building whose design was based on the Parthenon.

Smithfield Street Bridge at dawn.

St. Paul's Cathedral reflected in Carnegie Mellon University's Software Engineering Institute.

University of Pittsburgh's Cathedral of Learning.

Phipps Conservatory.

Carnegie Mellon Research Institute.

Chandelier in the Benedum Center for the Performing Arts.

Just blocks away stands one of the many gifts to the city from industrialist Henry Phipps — the Victorian-styled Phipps Conservatory. Upon its opening in 1893, the sensational plant and flower exhibits delighted visitors and continue to do so today. The glass pavilion roofs with their romantic curves create a beautiful backdrop for this, the largest greenhouse in the country, covering two and one-half acres.

Interior views are often more interesting than the outer shells of many buildings — the cool marble of Carnegie Music Hall, the medieval style of the Cathedral of Learning's Common Room, the Union Trust rotunda of Two Mellon Bank Center, the restored P&LE Railroad's Grand Concourse Restaurant, and the brilliant stained glass windows of Heinz Chapel.

Holy Spirit Catholic Byzantine Rite Church.

Heinz Chapel's stained glass windows.

Trinity Cathedral.

Rodef Shalom Temple.

St. Paul's Cathedral.

Sculpture in East Liberty.

Steelworker sculpture, North Shore Landing.

North Shore Landing.

Churches and synagogues have contributed as much to the culture of Pittsburgh as its architectural treasures. Dwarfed by the surrounding office buildings and skyscrapers downtown, the 1871 Trinity Cathedral and Graveyard has survived, along with some of the oldest graves in the city. Its neighbor, the 1905 First Presbyterian Church, boasts 14 Tiffany stained glass windows. The dome-topped Immaculate Heart of Mary Church, a Polish Hill landmark, was built by the parishioners themselves in 1904 after architect William Ginther's design. In Oakland, you will find the Rodef Shalom Temple, built in 1907, just a few blocks from the Gothic St. Paul's Cathedral, completed in 1906.

For adornment, Pittsburgh's collection of cooling fountains, statues and memorials are scattered in neighborhoods and squares around the city. In Allegheny Landing Park on the North Shore, the fluid sculpture is imbedded in the walkway and free-standing walls atop a grassy knoll, overlooking the Allegheny River. Also on the North Shore, in Roberto Clemente Park, stands the Allegheny County Vietnam Memorial. The dome was designed in the shape of an inverted hibiscus, a symbol of peace, and covers life-size statues of veterans in a homecoming pose.

Pittsburgh architectural landmarks add a dimension to the city that cannot be denied or ignored. They add to the city's value as reminders of the past and visions of the future. As functional beauty, these landmarks are to be enjoyed and treasured as part of the city's daily life.

Allegheny County Vietnam Veterans Memorial.

Stephen Foster Memorial statue.

CULTURE

Be it exquisite art, dance, theater, or musical expression, Pittsburgh's cultural scene has it all.

Pittsburgh's glowing display of galleries and performing arts defies the city's reputation as a tough, sports-crazed town. The uninitiated might be surprised, but those in the know recognize that Pittsburgh challenges the best in drama, music, dance, and art.

The internationally-acclaimed Pittsburgh Symphony Orchestra performs within the elegant Heinz Hall. Subscription holders are held mesmerized by evenings of music under crystal chandeliers. Opera buffs revel in the drama and sound of the Pittsburgh Opera Company. Tito Capobianco takes credit, and standing ovations, here.

Dance in the city has a strong foothold, and an ardent following. The Pittsburgh Ballet Theater is committed to commissioning new works from the nation's freshest and most original choreographers. Under the artistic direction of Patricia Wilde, the theater performs 19th-century masterpieces and exhibits a strong Balanchine influence.

Sculpture Hall, Carnegie Museum of Art.

Heinz Hall.

Clayton.

Benedum Center.

Children's Museum.

Modern dance has its champions in the likes of the Dance Alloy's contemporary repertory dance company, and the innovative cross-disciplinary performances of the Mary Miller Dance Company. The Pittsburgh Dance Council brings the world's best modern dance groups into town — from the most-acclaimed legends to the newest stars on the modern dance horizon.

The city's art scene is alive and diverse as well. A day's exploration of the city's galleries might uncover anything from 15th-century antique treasures to modern neon art; Alaskan collectibles to Japanese woodblock prints; limited edition lithographs to ready-to-wear fiber art.

The Carnegie Museum of Art, one of the five largest in the country, houses a permanent collection of Old Masters, French Impressionists, 19th- and early 20th-century American art, as well as an exciting collection of contemporary works. At the Frick Art Museum you can view paintings from Italian Renaissance to French Rococo, along with tapestries, bronze statuettes, and Chinese porcelain.

Carnegie Library, North Side.

Three Rivers Arts Festival.

Pittsburgh Center For The Arts.

Jazz Festival.

Art festivals are year-round events throughout the city, with the largest being the Three Rivers Arts Festival. This 17-day event fills the downtown with paintings and sculpture, strolling musicians, performing artists, and craftsmen in working exhibits. Other festivals are locally placed within neighborhoods — the Shadyside Summer Arts and Jazz Festival, Homewood's Harambee II Black Arts Festival, and the South Side Summer Street Spectacular.

For great drama, the Pittsburgh Public Theater, the area's largest fully-professional company, presents contemporary plays, world classics and new works. The Civic Light Opera brings broadway musicals into town, and the Three Rivers Shakespeare Festival performs a few of the Bard's best known plays each summer. Drama student productions from the theater departments of the nationally known Carnegie Mellon University, the University of Pittsburgh, and Point Park College add another dimension to an eclectic theater season that will keep you enthralled and coming back for more.

ILTON

DOWNTOWN

As the backdrop for Fortune 500 corporations, or a lesson in Early American history, the Golden Triangle shines.

Pittsburgh's downtown buzzes with the energy of a vital, thriving city. From its meager beginning as a French trading post, commerce and industry still keep the downtown area growing and strong.

At a time when most inner-city districts are being deserted for the suburban beltways, Pittsburgh's downtown has managed to sustain its central hold. The Golden Triangle maintains a government district, shopping area, banking and business center, all within a 15-minute walk. And with the exception of just a few streets, it's all within the original street plan laid out in 1784 (which explains some of the quirky intersections and odd little corners).

Part of the reason Pittsburgh has remained a downtown-focused center city has been its geographic location as it relates to transportation. Picture the metropolitan region as a wheel, with the downtown district as the hub. All of the routes, whether by rail, bridge, river, or road, worked out of the hub. There was virtually no way to get from one spoke to another — all routes led through downtown.

Pittsburgh skyline at night.

Fifth Avenue, downtown.

Strip District.

Even though the connecting roads have since been built, the downtown area continues to pull in crowds. Shoppers can stroll through the open-air produce paradise of the Strip District, along Penn Avenue and Smallman Street, where they'll find ethnic shops, fresh fish buys, bulk candy stores, and discount groceries. Or they could lose themselves in the department stores of Horne's, Kaufmann's, and Saks Fifth Avenue.

Downtown has its share of indoor malls too. The stunning glass atrium of One Oxford Center is filled with upscale shops and restaurants, as are the European-styled Arcade Shops at Fifth Avenue Place, and the retail section of PPG Place.

Entrance to the Golden Triangle.

Smithfield Street Bridge.

One Oxford Center.

The Point by day.

The Point by night.

PPG Food Court.

With five full-service hotels, a host of fine restaurants, the Cultural District, the David Lawrence Convention Center, and the Civic Arena all within easy walking distance of each other, visitors to the city needn't venture far. And just across the Monongahela River they'll find the revitalized Station Square, a popular night spot for dining, dancing, and shopping. Across the Allegheny River is Three Rivers Stadium, home to the Pirates and Steelers.

In the center of the Golden Triangle is Market Square, the only open space in the 1784 plans. Back then, it was called the Diamond, the Scottish word for place or square. Over time, a series of buildings were built on the space, until 1961 when the land was cleared to create the grassy square the city enjoys now.

Reflecting pool at Gateway Center.

Station Square.

Kaufmann's clock.

City County and One Mellon Bank Buildings.

Market Square.

Downtown business people.

Follow Forbes Avenue to Grant Street where you will find the Allegheny County Courthouse and Jail. Step back into the spacious inner courtyard, a cool, shaded retreat within the granite walls — the perfect escape from the noise of traffic and the bustle of the business lunch crowd.

The business crowd does *seem* to keep moving, but actually, the downtown workers seek out quiet spots like Mellon Square, the reflective space within PPG Place, the lush green of the indoor Wintergarden, and the shaded paths of Gateway Center.

Like every other aspect of Pittsburgh, the relaxed spots found between a hectic paced world contribute to the value of the downtown scene.

Walkway at Gateway Center.

View from Spring Hill.

Courtyard of the Allegheny County Courthouse and Jail.

Roberto Clemente Memorial Park.

NEIGHBORHOODS

Quaint ethnic storefronts, regal mansions, and period Victorian homes comprise a part of Pittsburgh's charm.

If the downtown is Pittsburgh's pulse and heartbeat, the neighborhoods are its soul. With more than 80 separate neighborhoods — each individual and distinct pockets of culture — Pittsburgh retains Old World ties and religious diversity. Many families have remained in the same areas for generations. You will find Italians in Bloomfield, Germans in Troy Hill, Jews in Squirrel Hill, and Poles on the flats of the South Side.

The North Side was originally the town of Allegheny, annexed to Pittsburgh in 1907. Old Allegheny, at the time, was a substantial industrial power in its own right. Its factories produced everything from cast iron bathtubs, glass, and locomotives, to textiles, carriages, and saddles. At the turn of the century, Millionaire Row was said to house more millionaires than any other two blocks in the world. The mansions are still there. They are presently the administration offices and classrooms of Allegheny County Community College.

Mission Street, St. Josaphat Church is in the photo.

Allegheny East.

North Side.

Elliot.

Blocks away are the brownstone fronts of the stately Mexican War Streets. During the past 20 years, these homes have been undergoing an almost magical restoration. The 20-block section has been purchased by urban pioneers, interested in retaining the old-style elegance of the outer shell, while incorporating modern design and convenience into the interior. Walking the tree-lined streets, you can almost imagine the horse-drawn carriages that once clattered along the cobblestones.

Bedford Square, South Side.

View of West End Bridge from North Side.

Sidney Street, South Side.

Mount Washington, Incline.

St. John the Baptist.

South Side.

The South Side shares a similar history, and a similar transformation. The factories here produced iron and glass. By the mid-1800s, old Birmingham, as it was called at the time, produced one-half of the country's glasswork. With the growth of industry and influx of immigrants at the turn of the century, the population increased steadily and quickly. Germans and Irish made their homes on the slopes, while Eastern Europeans squeezed into the flats in rowhouses between tiny streets. The Victorian storefronts are still in use, but now they are more likely to house art galleries, bookstores, jazz night clubs, antique shops, and restaurants. Like the rest of the city, the South Side is changing — from blue collar bars to upscale night spots.

Above the South Side towers the Mount Washington neighborhood with one of the greatest views of the city. For many years the steep hill was called "Coal Hill." The real estate on top wasn't valued as it is now. Back then, the smoke from ongoing coal fires and the heavy Pittsburgh industry didn't give much back in the way of beautiful scenery.

A little further down river is the West End. This neighborhood, too, contributed to Pittsburgh's glass production, plus the area had an oil refinery, iron mills, and saltworks. Local history remembers the town of Temperanceville, where a late 1830s experiment in prohibition failed miserably within ten years. Drive further into the hills to the West End Overlook, another spectacular vantage point that looks out over the Ohio River and straight into the downtown scene. It's a favorite spot to watch fireworks and photograph the city.

Mexican War Street area.

Squirrel Hill.

The East End was first populated by the industrialists wishing to get away from the dirt and noise of the city. It's almost laughable to think of Oakland, Shadyside, and Squirrel Hill as suburban properties. They are as vital to Pittsburgh as any other section. Oakland, in fact, is the third largest downtown in the state of Pennsylvania. The neighborhood bustles with university students from Carnegie Mellon University, the University of Pittsburgh, Chatham College, and Carlow College. A great health care and research network fills a good part of the area. Included are the transplant center of Presbyterian Hospital, Children's Hospital, Montefiore, Magee Womens Hospital, and the Eye and Ear Hospital.

Tourists from around the world, and across town, visit sights like The Carnegie Museum, the Frick Art Museum, and Phipps Conservatory. And you'll find historic homes like Clayton, the former home of Henry Clay Frick, now restored and open to the public.

Mexican War Street, North Side.

South Side, Slopes.

View of the City from the Slopes.

Craig Street, Oakland.

Shadyside.

Sewickley.

Shadyside is mostly residential, popular with the young professional crowd. Its shops and restaurants reflect the inhabitants — upscale and trendy. Squirrel Hill boasts larger homes, shaded streets and multi-ethnic markets and restaurants in the commercial district.

Pittsburgh neighborhoods maintain links to the past and hope for the future. The low cost of housing and comparatively low crime rate are an added bonus. Growing up surrounded by such close family and community ties, and a strong personal history, its's not difficult to understand the average Pittsburgher's hesitancy to ever leave the city they call home.

RIVERS

Pittsburgh's changing waterfront parallels the city's transition to sleek, high-tech town.

It's been said that Pittsburgh is a city that emerged from the rivers. And rightly so. In colonial times, rivers were an absolute necessity for an era when few modes of transportation were available. The triangle of land formed between the merging waters pointed out the direction for explorers and pioneers heading further inland: The Gateway to the West. Even now, Pittsburgh rivers see nearly 200,000 tons of freight move along its waters each year.

For many years, Pittsburgh used its rivers as another work horse, not only for transportation and power, but as a sewer for dumping industrial waste. However, as the city makes its move from manufacturing to a white collar center for research, health care, and technology, its rivers have been given the chance for rejuvenation. They are a growing source of pleasure for the people of Pittsburgh. A playground that, until a short time ago, had been left unused.

West End Bridge at sunset.

Pittsburgh skyline at dusk.

Fort Pitt Bridge.

Indians were responsible for naming the rivers. The Allegheny, forming the northern side of the point of land, means "Beautiful Water." The Monongahela flows on the southern side. Its name translates as "Falling Back." It's one of the few rivers in the world that runs in a south-to-north direction. Together they form the Ohio — simply put, "Something Great."

At the height of the steel industry's power, the "Mon" was flooded with chemicals, acids, and industrial run-off. It seemed to have an artificial blue cast to its water. At the Point where it met with the Allegheny, the difference in makeup was easily seen by the casual observer.

The Point at sunset.

The Point from the Ohio River.

Now that many mills have closed their doors, and with more stringent pollution legislation, the rivers have made a remarkable comeback in the past ten years. Game fish like walleye, bass, and sauger are being pulled in by local fishermen. Pleasure boat registration is at an all-time high. More boats are registered in Allegheny County than anywhere else in the country — 29,000.

Pittsburgh from the West End Overlook.

Duquesne Incline overlooking the Point.

The Seventh Street Bridge.

The River Belle passing the Point Park fountain.

A North Shore marina.

Marinas are filling the space along the river banks, adding restaurants with decks and glass front views to watch the river traffic. And even in cooler weather, you'll see a die-hard, rubber-suited water skier slicing a path through the water.

The vessels of the Gateway Clipper Fleet are a common sight. Designed with the majestic style of the Mississippi river boats of yesteryear, the two-story paddle boats, painted white and trimmed in red and black, attract tourists and locals on their river tours. Moonlight dance cruises are both romantic and exciting with the lights reflecting from the moving water.

Formula One raceboat in the Regatta competition.

The Majestic.

Bridges over the Allegheny River.

Smithfield Street Bridge.

Since closing the mills meant less freight traffic on the rivers, the waterways opened up for more leisure craft as convenient transportation possibilities. Baseball fans can dock at the wharf at Roberto Clemente Park. By boat you can reach a number of restaurants and even Sandcastle, the city's only waterslide park.

You can enjoy an evening concert while anchored at the Point, made even more relaxing as your craft gently rocks in the water. You become part of the scene, the boat's running lights one more reflection under the star-filled sky.

Fort Pitt Bridge.

"Anything That Can Float" entry in the Regatta celebration.

The Point Park Fountain at sunset.

PARKS

The city's dedication to its myriad parks contributes to Pittsburgh's high quality of life.

One of Pittsburgh's greatest blessings is the amount of green space interspersed throughout the city. It is believed to have more trees than any other city in the country. The cooling beauty of an urban forest adds immensely to a city's quality of life, providing shaded retreats, storm water control, natural air conditioning and purifying, wildlife shelter, and exquisite charm.

In part, the geography helps. Many of the steep, wooded slopes are protected from development simply because they are unsuitable for building.

A local interest in community forestry first began in the 18th century when William Penn required that of every five acres of land being cleared, one had to remain forested. The area continues to show a commitment to greenery with 177 parks, squares, and parklets in the city, and eight surrounding county parks.

West Park, North Side.

Heinz Hall Plaza.

Frick Park.

Schenley Park.

The most dramatic and easily recognized park would be Point State Park at the confluence of the Allegheny and Monongahela rivers. Here is where Pittsburgh history began, a history that strongly influenced the birth of this country, a history that parallels the struggles, successes, and spirit of the nation's growth in the past two centuries.

The park's 150-foot fountain, one of the world's largest man-made geysers, stands as a symbol of Pittsburgh's rebirth. Completed in 1974, the fountain jets 6,000 gallons of water per minute from the so-called fourth river — an aquifer 57 feet underground.

The city's oldest surviving structure, the Fort Pitt Blockhouse, is part of the park's attraction. Built in 1764 by the British Army, intent on building their most impervious fortification in the New World, the blockhouse still stands strong. Just a stone's throw away, you'll see the paved outlines of the French Fort Duquesne and the British Fort Pitt.

North Shore Landing.

Point State Park.

Nature Reserve.

Point Park is a regular destination for the Pittsburgh Symphony's occasional summer concerts. Other artists perform as well before a standing-room-only audience. This is the final stop for downtown parades, the finish line for the Great Race and Pittsburgh Marathon, the place to be for viewing exploding fireworks in the night sky. The park at the Point functions as a town square, leaving one to wonder how Pittsburgh got along without it all those years.

Opposite the Point, along the North Shore, is Roberto Clemente Memorial Park. Pittsburgh's most beloved baseball player is remembered with a beautiful sight next to Three Rivers Stadium — a grassy slope, curving walkway, and weeping willow trees bending gracefully to the water's edge.

The first formal provision for a city park system came in 1889 when Mary Croghan Schenley was persuaded to donate 300 acres of Oakland farmland to the cause. Schenley Park, located in the East End of Pittsburgh, enjoys a vibrant existence over one hundred years later. Housed within the heavily

Schenley Golf Course.

Highland Park Zoo.

Highland Park Zoo.

wooded acreage are a public golf course, the Victorian splendor of Phipps Conservatory, an ice skating rink, swimming pool, numerous baseball fields and tennis courts, and plenty of trees, trails, and benches.

The Highland Park Zoo competes for family recreation time as well. Having recently undergone a tremendous transformation, the animals are living comfortably in their natural environments — the Asian forest and African savanna. Kids have fun in the Children's Zoo where the friendly, smaller animals allow hands-on learning. Older brothers and sisters tend to prefer the shark tank in the Aqua Zoo or the bat cave of the darkened Twilight Zoo.

Several of the city's loveliest squares are downtown. Lunch-breaking office workers find the quiet of a mini-oasis just the mid-day pick me up they need. A bag lunch eaten in the Heinz Hall courtyard eases tension and cools a hot afternoon. Summer concerts are presented and enjoyed by all.

Pittsburghers have loved their parks for more than a century now. They picnic in them, jog their trails, nap under their leafy boughs, and revel in their green splendor. Pittsburgh parks are a big part of what makes Pittsburgh home.

Boyce Park.

Four-generation Pittsburgher Sally Webb was born and raised on the city's North Side. As associate editor of *Pittsburgh Magazine*, she often writes about her favorite city.

Photographer Walt Urbina has earned his reputation from a wide range of clients and projects. His photographs have appeared in numerous publications, including *Vanity Fair* and *Time* magazines. His versatile style translates easily from fashion to travel to corporate high tech.

Photographs in this book are available in prints for wall decor or for advertising through Photo Stock unlimited. Call: 412-242-5070 or 412-481-9650.